TEEN LIFE 411™

I'M SUICIDAL.
NOW WHAT?

JUDY MONROE PETERSON

ROSEN
PUBLISHING®

New York

Published in 2016 by The Rosen Publishing Group, Inc.
29 East 21st Street, New York, NY 10010

First Edition

Library of Congress Cataloging-in-Publication Data

Peterson, Judy Monroe.
I'm suicidal, now what?/Judy Monroe Peterson.
    pages cm. — (Teen life 411)
Includes bibliographical references and index.
ISBN 978-1-4994-6136-7 (library bound)
1. Teenagers—Suicidal behavior—Juvenile literature. 2. Suicidal behavior—Juvenile literature. 3. Suicide—Prevention—Juvenile literature. I. Title.
HV6546.P437 2016
362.28—dc23
2014040283

Manufactured in the United States of America

For many of the images in this book, the people photographed are models. The depictions do not imply actual situations or events.

CONTENTS

At times, many people feel as though the world is pulling them down and they just can't cope. This feeling of being overwhelmed by life's hurdles is especially common during the teen years, when new challenges, responsibilities, and pressures can pile up. Young people may also be facing problems with friends, at home or school, with bullying, or with an alcohol or drug addiction. In addition, difficult feelings might be complicated by a serious life event, including the separation or divorce of parents or the loss of a family member, friend, or even a beloved pet. It's no wonder that some individuals experience emotional overload, leading them to feel depressed, helpless, and hopeless.

If such distressing feelings continue over long periods of time, teens may feel isolated and separate themselves from everyone else. Some fall into deep despair and try drastic actions to escape their misery—including suicide, the act of intentionally taking one's own life. People who try to take their own lives usually do not want to die, but they see no alternatives to stop their endless mental and emotional suffering.

Suicide is found in every society. An enormous health problem, it ranks as one of the leading causes of death globally. The World Health Organization (WHO) reports that more than 800,000 people die from suicide every year, equaling about one death every forty seconds. Suicide is also a major concern in the United States. The Centers for Disease Control and Prevention (CDC) lists it as the

Everyone has different problems to overcome throughout life. After teens are past suicidal crises, they can get help understanding themselves and begin to build brighter futures.

tenth leading cause of death overall and the third leading cause of death for individuals aged ten to twenty-four. It is especially troubling that young people turn to suicide as the solution to their problems with alarming regularity. For every individual who dies by suicide, many others attempt it, and even more suffer the despair that leads them to even consider taking their own lives. Fortunately, it doesn't have to be this way.

Everyone needs help sometimes. Teens, who are navigating the challenging path between childhood and adulthood, should always feel free to ask for help, no matter how alone they feel or how hopeless things may seem. Depending on their situation, they can talk to a parent, a trusted adult or friend, a teacher, a school counselor, or a religious leader. Or they can turn to crisis hotlines to get immediate help. Health professionals often work with individuals who are suicidal to reduce their risk influences and strengthen factors that protect them. These protective features include healthy coping and problem-solving skills, learning to recognize and feel grateful for the positive aspects of their lives, improving family relationships, finding social support, and beginning psychotherapy or other mental health care options. Under proper medical care, prescription treatments such as antidepressants abate depression and actually eliminate suicidal thinking and behavior.

Though it may be difficult for young people to learn how to make the best of their circumstances and how to handle changes—both good and bad—the excellent news is that with time, effort, and, if necessary, assistance, they can develop a healthy, positive state of mind and the skills to meet everyday challenges and demands. The vast majority of teens who were once in great emotional pain go on to live happy and healthy lives. They feel a sense of hope for today and what lies ahead by learning from the past and moving on to brighter, wiser, more grounded futures.

UNDERSTANDING SUICIDE

Suicide is a choice made when sadness and despair combine with unclear thinking and the opportunity to take one's life. It is a decision that is final because the dead cannot come back to life. Unlike on a television show, when a character dies and then miraculously appears in another episode, real death is forever. Suicide is particularly tragic because it is preventable.

Threatening or attempting suicide is usually a plea for help. Troubled individuals may be signaling that they feel overwhelmed with unsolvable problems. Such behaviors often indicate that people have depression and can no longer handle their distressing feelings, thoughts, and stressful situations. They threaten or try to take their lives to end their great pain. Suicide, though, is never a good solution or end to any problem.

A suicidal teen feels isolated and in despair. His feelings, or emotions, influence all his thoughts, his actions, and his relationships with other people.

MAJOR GLOBAL PUBLIC HEALTH PROBLEM

Suicide has been recorded for more than two thousand years. In modern times, many different types of individuals have taken their own lives, including children, teens, and adults. Suicide continues to be a critical issue for today's societies around the globe and can have lasting, harmful effects on families, friends, and communities. The WHO reports that more people die each year from suicide than from all murders and wars added together. To look at this horrific information another way, one individual somewhere in the world takes his or her life every forty seconds. The exact numbers may differ because many countries have little or no record keeping on suicide. These figures do not include suicide attempts, which occur much more frequently than suicide. According to the WHO, more than twenty people attempt to take their lives for every one adult who dies from the act of suicide.

The rates of suicide vary widely among different cultures and age groups. Sadly, the worldwide rates among teens and young adults have risen faster than those in any other age group. The WHO ranks suicide as the second leading cause of death for people ages ten to twenty-four.

Age-standardized suicide rates (per 100,000 population), both sexes, 2012

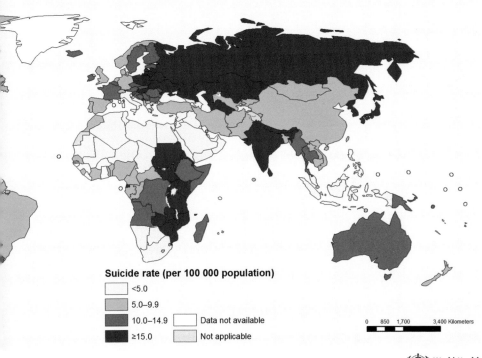

Suicide rate (per 100 000 population)

- <5.0
- 5.0–9.9
- 10.0–14.9
- ≥15.0
- Data not available
- Not applicable

0   850   1,700   3,400 Kilometers

World Health Organization

The boundaries and names shown and the designations used on this map do not imply the expression of any opinion whatsoever on the part of the World Health Organization concerning the legal status of any country, territory, city or area or of its authorities, or concerning the delimitation of its frontiers or boundaries. Dotted and dashed lines on maps represent approximate border lines for which there may not yet be full agreement.

Data Source: World Health Organization
Map Production: Health Statistics and Information Systems (HSI)
World Health Organization

To increase awareness of suicide, the WHO hosts a World Suicide Prevention Day (http://www.iasp.info/wspd) every September 10. Teens can participate in the Cycle Around the Globe event as well as local activities.

SERIOUS PROBLEM IN THE UNITED STATES

Throughout recent history, suicide has been one of the leading causes of death in the United States. In 2011, the CDC tallied more than thirty-nine thousand suicides, making it the tenth leading cause of death for Americans. That figure translates into a staggering 107 deaths by suicide every day. Looking closely at the statistics for young people is frightening. For youth between the ages of ten and twenty-four, suicide is the third leading cause of death, resulting in approximately 4,600 lives lost each year. Currently, the American Association of Suicidology estimates that someone under the age of twenty-five completes a suicide every two hours somewhere in the nation.

The number of suicides is probably higher than that because many go unreported. Sometimes suicides look like accidents. For example, the car crash of a single driver might be recorded as an accident. However, if law enforcement officials do not see skid marks on the road, the cause of death could be an autocide. Similarly, suicide may be disguised as an accidental drug overdose. Some teens take risks that skirt the edge of suicidal behavior, disregarding their own safety and that of others. They may perform dangerous feats or maneuvers in cars or on motorcycles. Or they might drive a vehicle without a seatbelt or ride a motorcycle without a helmet.

The CDC is working to monitor the problem of teen suicide and suicide attempts. The agency uses this information to develop programs for preventing such acts of despair and desperation.

Completed suicides are only part of this national health issue. Attempted suicides are another significant element. No official counts on the number of attempts exist, and many cases are not reported or treated by health professionals. However, the CDC estimates that at least one million people intentionally hurt themselves every year. That means as many as twenty-five attempts occur for each completed suicide.

The results from the 2011 Youth Risk Behavior Surveillance Survey System on teen suicide attempts are sobering. Out of a group of one hundred high school students, approximately sixteen young people said they had seriously thought about suicide during the past year, and eight had made a suicide attempt. The CDC conducts this survey nationwide every two years to monitor the health risks and behaviors of students in grades nine through twelve. Suicidal behavior is a major concern in today's society, and the problem is not going away.

SUICIDES INVOLVING OTHER PEOPLE

Suicide usually refers to an individual taking his or her own life. Although rare, sometimes other people are involved, such as in a suicide pact, group suicide, or murder suicide. A suicide pact is when two or more people agree to die together or at the

More than nine hundred people killed themselves in a mass suicide staged by members of the People's Temple and their leader, Jim Jones, in Georgetown, Guyana, on November 24, 1978.

same time using the same method. These arrangements are often between friends, within a family, or people in relationships.

Group suicide occurs when many people kill themselves together. They take these drastic means in search

of shared religious or spiritual beliefs, as a form of political protest, or to avoid military capture.

Some suicides accompany or follow a violent act, such as murder suicide, or homicide suicide, in which an individual takes the lives of other people before or while committing suicide, often with a gun. Suicide bombers are one example. They use explosives to kill as many people as possible, including themselves. These individuals often target a specific group for religious, moral, political, or cultural reasons, seeing their own deaths as acts of self-sacrifice. This book focuses only on individuals who think about or attempt to end their own lives.

CATEGORIES OF SUICIDE IDEAS AND BEHAVIORS

Suicidal behavior is a series of activities that takes many forms, including suicidal thinking, suicidal intent, preparing to commit suicide, suicide attempt, and completing suicide. Occasionally, some people vaguely think about sleeping forever or wishing to be dead, but they don't act on their thoughts. Suicidal intent occurs when suicidal thinking is accompanied by an intention to perform the act. For instance, teens may consider taking a large amount of pills to end their lives but then realize they would never go through with it.

The likelihood of serious danger rises when individuals prepare to commit suicide because they move into all-out

Some extremely despondent teens may think about taking their lives because they feel alienated from their families, friends, and peers. They may avoid seeking mental health care because they question their self-worth.

action. They may make an actual plan and find the methods and items needed to carry out their ideas. A number of young people might give away their prized possessions to others or say things like, "I won't be a burden any longer."

Suicide attempts are potentially self-injurious behaviors in which people try to take their own lives. Even if suicide is initiated, individuals might halt their activities because of self-reflection, or another person could stop the actions. Sometimes their plans do not work as intended. Teens may not experience any physical harm during their suicide attempts. Mild, moderate, or serious injuries may result in other situations. Completing suicide is the final, irreversible act that lasts forever.

LIFTING THE STIGMA

If a classroom of teens were asked, "What is more common in the United States, homicide (murder) or suicide?" the answer would probably be homicide. That response seems to make sense. People are aware of murders because the media regularly report about homicides on television and the Internet and in newspapers and magazines. Yet suicide occurs more than twice as often as homicide but is much less likely to appear in the headlines because it is an exceedingly uncomfortable topic for most individuals. Adults may find it difficult to understand and accept that young people could want to take their own lives. As a result, they might feel uncomfortable and avoid talking about suicidal feelings and behaviors, even with their own teenage children.

This strong taboo has led some people to cover up their desperate anguish and not seek appropriate help because of the stigma (disgrace or shame) that can be associated with suicide. They fear being thought of as weak, crazy, or cowardly. Fortunately, the stigma is lifting. Many international and national organizations and governments, as well as dedicated individuals, realize that suicide is a serious health issue and are working together to raise awareness of suicide and its prevention. Today, suicide help and treatment is widely available.

COMPLICATIONS

Suicidal thoughts and actions take an emotional toll on people who want to take their own lives. They lose the ability to function effectively on a daily basis. Often, they get tunnel vision and focus their thoughts on end-of-life plans, to the exclusion of life around them: lives, including aspects of them that may well actually be positive. In their distress, they may attempt suicide, but this action could lead to unexpected and grim consequences. Even if individuals get to a hospital and have immediate medical care after harming themselves, they could have serious damage to the liver, heart, or kidneys. Slashing the wrists leaves scars and may permanently affect the use of the hands. Sometimes disfigurement, brain injuries, partial or full paralysis, or a permanent coma occurs. Someone could become physically handicapped for life. Tragically, death can also result.

When a teen takes his or her life, many people are affected. Suicide survivors are the devastated and grieving parents, siblings, friends, and other people who were close to the young person. They often grapple with intense feelings of shock, denial, guilt, abandonment, sadness, and anger. Some survivors may blame themselves for not recognizing the teen's despair or for failing to help. Other individuals can feel guilty because the suicide appeared to have been caused by a specific event, such as a humiliation or rejection, in which the survivor played a part.

The impact of suicide on the family can be enormous, as each person struggles with his or her own grief in his or her own way. For the family to come together and heal, everyone needs to begin talking to each other and sharing their emotions. Going to a bereavement (grief) group or seeing a therapist may bolster emotional well-being.

CHAPTER 2

Presuicidal behaviors represent a plea for help by teens who do not know how to cope with their misery. Such actions are not typical responses to the daily stresses encountered by most people. Determining who may become suicidal is difficult because no single risk factor exists. However, certain multiple elements can increase the risk for death by suicide.

UNDERSTANDING RISK FACTORS

One significant risk factor for suicide is depression. More than half of teens who are suicidal are considered clinically depressed. Young people at high risk of taking their lives may be very socially isolated or depressed. Alcohol and drug abuse are also major components of suicide. However, just because you have one or more of these risk factors does not mean you will fall into making the desperate choice of suicide.

Here are some of the main risk factors for teen suicide:

- Alcohol and drug abuse
- Bullying and cyberbullying
- Depression
- Emotional, physical, or sexual abuse

- Exposure to other suicides
- Family history of depression
- Gambling
- Homelessness
- Transitions such as moving, changing schools, or parental divorce

Some teens are homeless or live in unfit housing, which puts them at higher risk of suicide. The Sasha Bruce House in Washington, D.C., provides various services for homeless young people.

- Problems at school
- Problems with family, friends, or in other relationships
- Prior suicide attempt
- Lesbian, gay, bisexual, or transgender
- Unplanned pregnancy

Alcohol and Drug Abuse

Some young people turn to alcohol and drugs to help them forget about their problems or cope with feelings of pain, fear, or depression. Others might use these substances to deal with the enormous pressure to perform well at school and in athletics or to meet family expectations. Alcohol and substance abuse are high-risk behaviors because they impair judgment and can allow individuals to act on self-destructive feelings that they might not otherwise respond to. The CDC ranks alcohol and drug abuse second only to depression as the most frequent risk factor for suicidal thoughts and attempts.

At first, alcohol may elevate the mood, but soon its true nature as a depressant takes over as someone continues to drink. It quickly affects the brain and nervous system and all other systems in the body. Although teens might feel they are escaping from feelings of sadness when they drink, alcohol use affects their vision, speech, memory, coordination, judgment, and response time. They are more likely to perform poorly in school, athletics, or work and have much higher odds of traffic accidents.

Drug abuse includes misusing legal medicines or using illegal drugs or other chemicals. People who get caught up in substance abuse tend to have low self-esteem and are depressed and stressed. As their use continues, they often withdraw from family and friends, become socially isolated, and do poorly at school. Like alcohol, substance abuse can increase impulsiveness and

Teens who turn to alcohol and illegal drugs to get away from their painful situations and emotions are at greater risk of committing suicide. Substance abuse never solves anyone's problems.

decrease inhibitions, making teens more likely to act on suicidal thoughts and behaviors.

Bullying and Cyberbullying

Bullying is when someone or a group of people do or say hurtful things repeatedly to gain power over an individual. Being bullied involves name-calling, pushing, or hitting. Bullies can ignore, isolate, or exclude someone from social activities. Sometimes they steal or break things that a victim owns.

Some bullies embarrass, harass, or threaten people using computers, smartphones, and other technology. This type of bullying is called cyberbullying, and it happens through unwanted and harmful e-mails, texting,

A target of continual bullying may feel isolated and degraded. He may come to believe that the only way out of his helpless and hopeless life is to end it.

instant messaging, wall posts, blogs, websites, or interactive games. Cyberbullies use words or pictures to embarrass or taunt individuals at home, school, or anywhere. They may spread rumors and lies, tease or scare their victims, tell secrets, or send embarrassing videos of individuals to others or post them on social media. Victims of cyberbullying may feel they can never escape the constant harassment and humiliation.

Any type of bullying is extremely upsetting and painful for those who experience it. They may feel trapped, isolated, helpless, or unsafe. Severe depression and anxiety can set in. If victims of bullying are unable to cope with these damaging effects, the tragic result can be bullycide, suicide committed as a result of being bullied.

Teen Gambling

Teen gambling is a major problem in the United States, whether it's betting on football, basketball, or other sports games or playing poker or card games. Young people might sneak into casinos or use bookies or gambling websites. Sometimes they stay up all night playing online or at parties.

Gambling may seem like an easy way to relieve stress. At first, some gamblers may make money. But most do not foresee the cycle of occasionally winning and more often losing and going into serious debt. They may steal money from family members, never repay loans from friends, or ring up high credit card bills. Frightened teen gamblers can become isolated and depressed. If they slide into hopelessness, their risk of suicide greatly rises.

Families and Stress

For many teens, adolescence is a time of experimentation and change. They need and want independence, which can sometimes lead to family squabbles. This struggle may be difficult at times, but it's a normal part of growing up. However, continual, intense fighting with parents can turn into major, ongoing battles, and communication often breaks down. Young people who constantly feel misunderstood and unloved might become severely depressed.

During the teen years, young people begin to pull away emotionally and mentally from their parents, which can lead to conflict. Teens may become depressed over intense arguments about dating, curfews, and responsibilities.

Sometimes stress within the family rises when major changes occur, such as divorce, job loss, issues with finances and health, or loss of a family member. Some teens may live in appalling family environments. Perhaps a teen has a neglectful parent because the mom or dad has a serious problem with alcohol or drug abuse. Or a teen could be emotionally, physically, or sexually abused by a family member. Young people who suffer chronic abuse at home or witness domestic violence are more likely to be fearful, be depressed, and think about killing themselves than others who do not experience such cruelty.

Relationship Problems

Adolescence is usually a time of trying different romantic relationships. Breaking up, making up, and breaking up again can be painful, but it's part of the process of becoming emotionally mature. Some teens do not cope well with these ups and downs. After a breakup, a teen like this may feel his or her world has collapsed and life is not worth living without that special person. There have been cases in which teens of both genders have attempted suicide after the end of a relationship.

Friendships often take on great importance during the teen years, which is also the time when young people search for identities and a sense of belonging. Having friends is vital. A

group of friends can become very close and seem like a family. Teens who do not belong to a group or develop close friendships may feel lonely, angry, or depressed. If their sad feelings become overwhelming, they may think about suicide or make attempts.

Everyone has the need to belong and be valued as a member of a group. Teens can meet their social needs in positive ways that benefit themselves and people with whom they are connected.

Problems at School

As teens mature, they undergo many social, physical, and emotional changes. Sometimes they feel moody during these years. That's normal. They may also feel a lot of pressure to do well academically, get into college, join a club, star on a sports team, or just fit in. It's a lot to handle. Many young people do fine over these years, even with a few bumps along the way.

Sometimes young people have great trouble with school. They may be emotionally withdrawn from their classmates, skip school often, and do poorly on schoolwork and tests. Their problems may come from having a learning disability, attention-deficit disorder, or a behavioral issue. Continued academic frustrations can evolve into feelings of deep sadness. In contrast, some young people feel highly pressured to do well at school. They can sink into despair when they fail to meet their goals or worry that disaster is just around the corner. This constant sense of fear and anxiety can result in depression and suicidal thoughts and actions.

WARNING SIGNS OF SUICIDE

Most suicidal people, including teens, usually show various warning signs of suicide. Recognizing these signs in oneself or others can mean the difference between life and death. Here are some warning signs:

- Direct statements such as "I want to die," "I don't want to live anymore," "I just want to go to sleep and never wake up," or "I wish I were dead."

- Indirect statements such as "They'll be sorry when I'm gone" or "Soon this pain will be over."
- Depression
- Withdrawal from family, friends, and social activities
- Preoccupation with talking, writing, drawing, or listening to songs about death
- Giving away prized possessions
- Excessive moodiness, including crying and anger
- Increased aggressive or impulsive behavior, such as violent outbursts or running away from home
- Engaging in alcohol and drug use, reckless driving, or other risky behavior
- Previous suicide attempt
- Sudden cheerfulness, which can signal a decision to attempt suicide

A Closer Look at Depression

Everyone feels sad sometimes during life's setbacks or losses or may feel blue or unhappy for short periods without reasons or warning. These feelings are normal and usually last a few hours or days. But if these feelings continue for weeks or longer or impair daily life, it may indicate that a person has a depressive disorder. The severity and duration are characteristics that separate ordinary sadness from depression. Mental illness, particularly depression, is a significant risk factor for suicide. Although highly treatable, depression is the leading cause of suicide among teens and adults. It's important to understand that the vast majority of people who are depressed do not commit suicide.

Major Depression

Major depression, also known as clinical depression, is a serious condition that requires treatment. People feel deeply sad for more than two weeks, which affects their ability to concentrate, perform well at school or work, or cope with everyday decisions and challenges. Sometimes they sleep too much or experience insomnia. Teens may significantly lose or gain weight. If untreated, depression can cause people to seriously think about and attempt suicide.

Seasonal Affective Disorder

Often called the "winter blues," seasonal affective disorder (SAD) makes people feel sad and tired during the winter months, when the hours of sunlight decrease. During this time, they may sleep and eat too much and withdraw from friends and social activities. Sad feelings usually lift in the spring and summer.

Dysthymia

This mild form of depression lasts two or more years. It can make it difficult for individuals to remember better times or enjoy their lives, although they may have occasional mood lifts.

Ongoing problems in school can be a warning sign of serious issues. Some teens may feel depressed because they do not know how to start or break into a group.

Bipolar Disorder (Manic Depressive Disorder)

Bipolar disorder is a serious illness. People experience radical emotional changes and mood swings, from manic highs to depressive lows. During manic periods, they may not sleep much, have great energy, feel extremely happy, and be full of ideas. Sometimes they are impulsive and spend money freely or use alcohol or drugs. Then they crash into depression and feel exceedingly sad, withdrawn, and unmotivated. During the depressive period, some people get so low that they may attempt suicide or take their own lives. If left untreated, these cycles tend to get worse over time.

Self-Injury and Suicide

Some individuals cut, burn, or hit themselves. By harming themselves, they temporarily release intense feelings of anger, anxiety, and pain, which cause them to feel real or alive. Most people who engage in self-injury act alone and try to hide their actions from others. Self-harm may or may not be a warning sign of suicide. It's definitely not healthy behavior. Anyone who feels like hurting himself or herself—or who has already started—should get help. Teens can approach someone they trust and share their feelings. Taking this step can help them get on the road to finding healthier ways to handle painful feelings.

WARNING SIGNS OF DEPRESSION AND BIPOLAR DISORDER

Warning signs of depression and bipolar disorder, including the severity and duration, vary for everyone. Signs of depression include the following:

- Persistent sadness and anxiety
- Feeling sad, hopeless, helpless, anxious, or worthless
- Little or no energy; feeling tired
- Problems concentrating or making decisions
- Withdrawal from family, friends, hobbies, and social activities
- Increased or decreased appetite
- Oversleeping or difficulty sleeping
- Irritability, anger, worry, extreme restlessness
- Frequent thoughts of suicide or death

Here are some signs of mania:
- Very energetic, happy, and talkative
- Extreme irritability; aggressive behavior
- Decreased need for sleep, but not feeling tired
- Feeling very important and having grand ideas
- Racing speech and thoughts
- Impulsive; poor judgment; easy to distract
- Reckless or rude behavior

MYTHS AND FACTS

MYTH

Most suicides happen without warning.

FACT

The majority of people who die from suicide have given warning signs of their intentions for a period of time.

MYTH

Talking about suicide gives someone ideas about committing suicide.

FACT

Talking openly and honestly about suicide can give a distressed individual great comfort and relief. Caring friends can make a critical difference in the person's life.

MYTH

Everyone who commits suicide leaves a note.

FACT

Most people do not leave suicide notes. If they do, their notes seldom contain reasons that explain their suicide.

CHAPTER 3

Life is full of problems, losses, and other difficult situations. Teens might experience breakups or continual rejection; testing and college-prep stress; the stress of not having enough money for college; and the stress of balancing school life, home chores, and after-school work. Some people can tackle various issues and move on with their lives, while others feel overwhelmed with their situation and become seriously depressed. They may lose hope for the future and mistakenly think suicide is a solution instead of an irreversible error.

There is no typical suicidal personality. Aside from depression or other mental illnesses, suicidal actions may be associated with many other causes, such as age, gender, ethnicity, and culture. Some teens might feel shame or embarrassment or fear alienation by family, friends, or classmates if they reveal their sexual orientation. Other possible factors could include personality traits, environmental influences, and, perhaps, some type of genetic connection.

WHO IS AT RISK?

Most teens who commit suicide are white males. In 2014, the CDC reported that teenage boys are four times as likely as teenage girls to commit suicide, but girls are much more likely to have suicidal thoughts and attempt suicide. The difference is probably because males tend to use more violent methods to kill themselves, such as firearms. In contrast, women may take extra doses of medications, which poison the body. If brought to the hospital emergency room in time, some people are saved, but others misjudge the dangers of the substance and take an overdose that results in lifelong disability or, tragically, death.

Researchers are trying to determine possible reasons for other teen suicide rates. This information helps to develop effective suicide prevention methods for different populations. For instance, suicide is the second leading

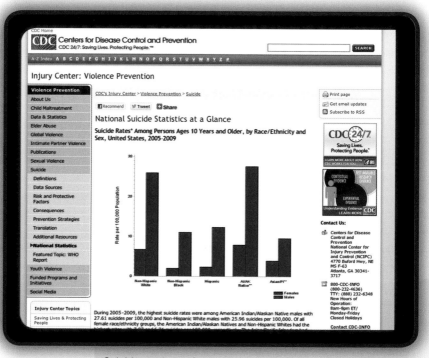

Suicide statistics for young people in the United States point to startling differences. For example, the Native American and Alaskan native populations have exceedingly high suicide rates compared to other ethnicities.

cause of death for American Indians and Alaska Natives ages fifteen to thirty-four. Based on the 2011 Youth Risk Behavior Surveillance Survey System, the CDC said that of students in grades nine through twelve, significantly more Hispanic female students reported attempting suicide in the last year than African American female students and white female students. Another finding is that, as a group, lesbian, gay, and bisexual youth experience more suicidal behavior than other youth.

AN AT-RISK TEEN'S PATH TO SURVIVAL

Elliott, a seventeen-year-old gay teen, shared his attempt to commit suicide with Dallas Voice, a site for lesbian, gay, bisexual, and transgender (LGBT) people in Texas. Elliott tried to commit suicide at age fifteen after enduring years of bullying from his peers. Some male students at his high school in the small town of Ennis, Texas, considered his passion for ballet dancing unusual, and they verbally and physically abused him for being different. At home, his brother, a drug abuser, and stepfather constantly tormented him about being gay. Feeling isolated and overwhelmed with despair, Elliott considered suicide and tried to take his life by using prescription drugs. He lived, but going through such a drastic decision frightened him into taking action.

After opening up to his mom, the teen's life began to improve in many ways. His abuse at home ended when his mom and stepfather divorced and his brother stopped using drugs. Elliott also became involved with Youth First Texas, an LGBT organization in Dallas. There, the teen joined a survivors group, which helps members focus on positive ways to handle stress. He tells young people who are thinking about suicide, "Whatever you're going through, it just makes you a stronger person. Whatever you go through makes you capable of doing things others can't."

PATTERNS OF SUICIDE OCCURRENCE

In recent years, scientists have discovered certain patterns that seem to be predictors of suicides. For example, some people without strong family or social contacts have a higher than average risk of taking their lives. They may be single, divorced, or widowed.

According to the U. S. Center for Health Statistics, suicide rates are lowest in December and the highest in the spring and fall. No one yet knows why this happens. Sometimes the media reports that suicide rates peak during the holidays or birthdays, but various research studies show that is not true. Such misinformation is of concern because it can interfere with possible suicide prevention efforts. Experts do not yet know why seasonal variations of suicide occur. Some scientists are researching the effects of seasonal changes on levels of hormones and neurotransmitters in the body.

The results of a 2014 study published in the scientific journal *Sleep* indicated that suicides are more likely to happen after midnight when people have insomnia. Based on these findings, scientists hope to investigate if treating insomnia helps reduce the risk of suicide.

COMMON TRAITS

Researchers find that people who take their lives have some traits in common. However, having these characteristics does not mean a person will become suicidal. The reasons for suicide are complex and very different for each individual who thinks or attempts self-destructive action.

Low Self-Esteem

Everyone has occasional days in which he or she feels low about himself or herself. But these negative feelings usually don't last long and fade away. Most teens have healthy self-esteem and feel confident and valued. They see themselves in a positive yet realistic way and usually take failure or mood swings in stride and move forward. In contrast, individuals with low self-esteem may dislike themselves, feel inferior to others, or believe they have no place or purpose in the world.

Self-destructive behaviors and activities may be symptoms of a more passive or indirect suicidal impulse and, certainly, of depression. Some teens act like they are trying to hurt themselves by engaging in reckless behavior. Risk takers might drink and drive, not use a seatbelt, or perform dangerous feats or maneuvers in cars or on motorcycles. Individuals might carry a gun and show off by mishandling it or pointing it at themselves and pretending to pull the trigger. Abusing alcohol or drugs damages both physical and mental health. Depression is usually a significant part of serious eating disorders, including anorexia (self-starvation), bulimia (overeating and then vomiting to force food out of the body), and compulsive overeating. Fortunately, eating disorders, like depression, are almost always treatable.

SELF-DESTRUCTIVE BEHAVIORS

Loneliness

Loneliness is the feeling of not being important or accepted by family, friends, peers, or other people. Some teens say they feel forlorn and empty even when with friends. Students with a physical or learning disability may feel alone because peers shun them. People can isolate themselves with alcohol or drugs. Sometimes individuals do not develop any close friendships. Lonely young people who feel their lives have no meaning and cannot connect with other people are at a higher risk of suicide.

Difficulty Expressing Emotions

Everyone experiences losses and disappointments at times. When events like these happen, people may feel rejected, upset, stressed, or depressed. Some teens are afraid to share their real emotions with trusted adults or friends. Instead, they cover up their feelings and let their rage or desperation build up inside. Over time, they can become depressed and vulnerable to suicidal actions.

Pessimists tend to view negative events as permanent and far-reaching. They can develop a more positive outlook on life by reminding themselves that no matter what happens to them, there is always hope.

Easily Angered

Some people lack self-control. They become angry easily and are quick to fight over perceived wrongs. They seldom react calmly or logically when difficult situations arise and may express their rage and frustrations in aggressive and violent ways. This can put them at a higher risk of getting physically hurt, resulting in death. Research shows that if firearms are available, highly enraged, impulsive individuals in crisis may use them to attempt suicide.

Perfectionism

Trying to do a good job at school and work is important, of course. However, young people who feel the need to be perfect constantly put themselves under undue pressure and have an overwhelming fear of failure. Meeting these relentlessly high standards becomes highly stressful. When they don't meet their impossible goals, they can become frustrated, extremely depressed, and sometimes suicidal.

Pessimism

Some people are optimists. Others are pessimists. Optimists believe in themselves, feel competent, and see problems as challenges that have solutions. They look at the world positively, welcome opportunities, and find ways to be successful. In contrast, pessimists have a more negative view of the world and see little hope for success. They give up easily when problems arise, and if they are overwhelmed, they may be more likely to have suicidal thoughts and behaviors.

DEVELOPMENT OF SUICIDAL BEHAVIOR

The vast majority of teens who deal with difficult life circumstances such as poverty, homelessness, abuse, or a family suicide go on to become healthy, strong, successful adults. Other people in similar situations develop major depression that, if untreated, could become suicidal. Scientists cannot yet fully explain why these two different life paths occur, but they believe complex and multiple factors cause suicidal behavior.

Some research indicates that suicide has a genetic component. For instance, biological children of someone with major depression or who has attempted or committed suicide are more likely to become depressed and possibly suicidal. Scientists think this means the occurrence of depression and the tendency toward developing suicidal behaviors may be influenced by someone's genes. It's important to understand that if genetic factors do exist, individuals are only predisposed to suicide—it does not mean they will end up taking their own lives.

Family history and circumstances may sway exceedingly stressed or depressed teens toward strong

People who live in unhealthy environments may be experiencing abuse, rejection, neglect, or other intense negative treatment. Such experiences can leave individuals with emotional scars and serious depression.

thoughts of suicide. Psychological problems, such as addictive and abusive behaviors by parents, are more likely to be present in the families of suicidal teens than in the families of other young people. Such dysfunctional families may teach wrong lessons about how to cope with daily living and fail to provide necessary security and emotional support and love for their children or teens. Some angry or depressed parents constantly use sharp criticism or harsh threats or punishments in the home. Their children can grow into fearful teens who constantly expect bad things to happen to them. In these abusive environments, they might become deficient in the coping and problem-solving skills necessary to deal with the challenges of growing up, which can lead to depression and, possibly, to suicide.

CHAPTER 4

Young people who are suicidal usually hide their feelings of despair and desperation from others for fear of being rejected, belittled, or dissuaded from taking their lives. They often feel isolated and believe they cannot find someone willing to help them. It's essential that teens who are thinking about hurting themselves or ending their lives keep themselves safe. Even if it feels scary or distressing, they absolutely need to tell someone about their suicidal feelings or plans immediately. Young people who are depressed and thinking of suicide do not need to go through difficult times afraid and alone. They can get help no matter where they live, anytime, day or night. They should try to remember that suicide is a permanent, irreversible solution for a temporary problem.

There are many different avenues that troubled youth can take to get help and tell someone about their emotional pain and problems. Teens may want to start with a parent or guardian, religious leader, friend's parent, teacher, or coach. These adults can give guidance about what to do next. Young people can also contact a suicide crisis center hotline or make an appointment with a doctor or mental health expert. Talking about suicidal behavior may be frightening and painful. But it's important to open up and be honest with whomever you talk with and ask for help.

In 2012, a sixteen-year-old unnamed teen in Wyoming, Ohio, talked to a Cincinnati television station about his three suicide attempts, at the ages of eight, eleven, and fourteen. The young person shared his experiences in the hope of helping other suicidal students. His peers tormented and taunted him, starting in grade school. He bottled up his emotional pain, feeling more and more alone, because he believed no one at home or in school wanted to listen to his thoughts. In great distress, he set suicide plans in motion but resisted taking his life three times. He told interviewer Kareem Elgazzar, "What ultimately stopped me from doing it was seeing the faces of the people who would horribly miss me. I knew that I had people to protect in my life, like my mom and my little sister—I knew that they needed me and so I just I knew I had to be there." At age fifteen, he attended a suicide prevention program at school that encouraged students to talk to a trusted adult. Afterward, he spoke with his mom, who listened and was supportive. The teen and his family now keep communications open with individual and family counseling.

GET IMMEDIATE HELP IF SUICIDAL

Teens who have just attempted suicide or are in crisis and think they may harm themselves must get medical attention immediately. They need to call 911 for emergency medical services or go directly to the local hospital emergency department. Also, witnesses to a suicide attempt should call 911 and ask for help.

Young people thinking about suicide may feel they cannot talk to anyone about their true feelings. Instead, they hide their agony and deep sadness from others. Teens may see suicide as a choice if their silent pain becomes unbearable—but they do not need to suffer alone. They can turn to a variety of free and confidential services to get help before taking any negative actions.

One important resource is the National Suicide Prevention Lifeline hotline at (800) 273-8255, which operates 24/7. All calls are routed to a local crisis center that makes referrals for anyone who needs help. The National Suicide Prevention Lifeline also manages the Lifeline Crisis Chat, which provides immediate support through chatting. This service operates from 2 p.m. to 2 a.m. Eastern Time seven days a week. People who answer the phones or chats are

caring, trained listeners and familiar with many different kinds of problems. Teens can talk about their feelings of isolation, fear, anger, or depression and get referrals for help. They can call or chat again if they

Sources of Strength, an organization in Denver, Colorado, holds sessions at high schools aimed at preventing youth suicide, and substance abuse, and teaching students to cope with life's challenges.

feel suicidal or just need someone to talk to about their issues.

Another crisis resource is the Jason Foundation's free smartphone app "A Friend Asks," which can be downloaded on iPhone or Android smartphones at any time. Teens can use the "Get Help Now" button on the app to reach a skilled chat specialist immediately. The Jason Foundation works to prevent youth suicide through its school programs.

Teens can also get help by texting. If in crisis, they can immediately talk with skilled counselors by using the toll-free Crisis Text Line (CTL). To use this service, text "CTL" to 741741. CTL is available nationwide every day of the year, at any time.

Some crisis resources focus on specific groups of people. The Trevor Project provides crisis intervention and suicide prevention services to gay, lesbian, and bisexual youth. The Trevor Helpline is a twenty-four-hour free suicide hotline at (866) 488-7386. Young people can also use TrevorChat, an online crisis chat service open six

Actress Jane Lynch speaks at a national Trevor Project event in New York City. This nonprofit organization promotes acceptance of gay, lesbian, bisexual, and transgender teens, with a focus on suicide-prevention programs.

hours a day. Members of the military can get free, immediate, confidential help by calling the Military Crisis Line at (800) 273-8255 and selecting 1. They

TELLING PARENTS HOW YOU FEEL

It's not always easy for parents to accept the idea that their teen is thinking about suicide and needs help. Some parents may have difficulty believing their son or daughter is suicidal. They may say that your feelings are what any teen goes through or that your thoughts of suicide will disappear. Individuals may have negative ideas about mental health care and do not believe therapists and therapy are helpful. Sometimes parents might not really listen to their teen and say things such as, "What are you complaining about?" or "There's nothing wrong with you." Before you tell your parents that you feel suicidal and need help, it's useful to think about what you want to say to them and then practice it beforehand. Stay calm as you speak, and be brief. Teens can also find information on local mental health resources and give that information to their parents. If your parents will not or cannot help, you need to immediately find someone else to help.

can also chat online with a Military Crisis Line specialist or send a text to 838255.

GETTING PROFESSIONAL HELP

Individuals who are suicidal can obtain help no matter where they live. They may call, chat, or text a crisis center hotline or make an appointment with a family doctor or mental health professional. Other options include talking to a school counselor, social worker, or psychologist. These people are trained in suicide interventions and can help in finding a therapist. Teens can do their own research to locate a mental health specialist by searching the Internet for local clinics and contacting them. Some hospitals have specialized clinics for youth dealing with depression and suicide. Talking with any of these professionals is a wise step toward learning how to pull out of despair and begin building a path toward a happy and healthy life.

Diagnosed by a Professional

Getting a correct diagnosis by a professional is critical for finding the best treatments to deal with suicidal thoughts and behaviors. A medical doctor is usually the first health professional someone sees. The physician will conduct a physical exam and laboratory tests to rule out some physical illnesses. For example, although depression is the most common cause of suicide, it's also a typical symptom of various thyroid disorders. The thyroid produces hormones that control the rate of many activities, including how fast the heart beats and how quickly the body uses up energy. Luckily, thyroid hormone replacement drugs are readily available.

Next, the physician records the medical history of the teen, including any family history of depression or suicide. He or she will ask questions about physical and mental health, major life changes or stresses, and thoughts of death or suicide. Prior suicide attempts or alcohol or illegal drug use should be honestly discussed. Disclosing

all prescription or over-the-counter drug use is also essential because certain ones can cause suicidal feelings, especially in young people.

Many times, suicidal thoughts or actions are linked to a mental health issue that is very treatable, such as depression. If this is the case, young people may need to see a psychiatrist or psychologist experienced in working with teens who can determine the causes of suicidal thinking and best treatment options. These mental health professionals usually start by conducting an assessment, which is a discussion between the teen and specialist.

The process of obtaining a mental health disorder diagnosis, such as major depression, can provoke strong reactions. Teens often find that putting a name to their experiences can be empowering.

The specialist may consult a teen's parents or guardians and other people close to the individual, school reports, and earlier medical or mental health evaluations. Finally, the psychiatrist or psychologist evaluates all of the information and makes a diagnosis.

Sometimes teens set up a medical appointment but become extremely upset or despondent before then. Staying safe is their top priority. They can ask a parent or another trusted adult for help or contact a suicide crisis line during the waiting period. If young people are afraid of hurting themselves, they need to call 911 or get to their local hospital emergency room immediately.

AFTER A DIAGNOSIS

Obtaining an evaluation and diagnosis by a mental health specialist is the first step toward finding the best treatment. To get a therapist, people usually need a referral, which often comes from a medical doctor. Treatments are usually on an outpatient basis. Fees for therapists vary widely depending on many factors, including the coverage provided in a family's health insurance plan. Some care may be free and covered by state or federal programs. It's a good idea for teens and their parents to discuss the costs for treatments.

The goal of treatment is getting people to function every day without thinking of suicide. Many different kinds of treatment are available. Therapists tend to favor one kind over another and tailor a plan for each individual. Young people might want to try several treatments to find what works best for them.

Saving Someone's Life

Sometimes, a friend of a troubled teen may pick up on suicidal signs before parents, teachers, or other adults. Red flags could include talking about being worthless or a burden on other people, suicide, or death; use of alcohol or drugs; acting recklessly, such as drinking and driving; declining performance in academics or sports; or withdrawing from family or friends. Individuals might give up activities they once enjoyed, such as music, sports, or clubs. Other troubling signals are giving away valued belongings, neglecting personal hygiene, exhibiting rapid mood swings, and saying goodbye to family and other people. Any signs of suicidal thoughts and behaviors must be taken seriously.

If someone appears in immediate danger of suicide, it's essential to stay with the person and immediately call 911, a crisis hotline, a local hospital emergency room, the teen's family doctor, or a trusted adult. You should try to keep the individual talking until help arrives. Any information about alcohol or drug use needs to be given to the emergency team. A friend of the suicidal teen can alert a parent, school counselor, or other trusted adult.

If the individual seems suicidal but is not in crisis, two things are critical: listen and get help. First, teens need to talk to their friend. A direct approach is best. In a calm manner, teens can briefly express their concerns and let the individual know they want to help by asking, "Have you been thinking about suicide?" or "Are you planning to commit suicide?" If the answer is yes, ask why and listen carefully, without acting judgmental. Just talking to someone who cares can help ease a troubled person's feelings of despair or acute sadness.

Someone who is suicidal often believes that no one cares about him or her. Actively listening to a friend and showing empathy can help an individual feel safe enough to express deep feelings freely.

Second, teens should encourage their troubled friends to talk with trusted adults or health professionals as soon as possible. The individual may refuse to take this step. In that case, you should go to a parent, guardian, school counselor, coach, nurse, religious or youth center leader, or another responsible adult who can get help. Your friend may feel angry for the breach of confidentiality, but someone who is suicidal needs professional care, even if suicide is not imminent. It's always better to risk losing a friend than a life.

Sometimes people post suicidal comments, illustrations, photographs, videos, or other content on social media, such as Facebook. If a post on Facebook appears suicidal, individuals can flag it and complete an online form. The user then receives an email from Facebook's safety team that includes the National Suicide Prevention Lifeline telephone number and a link. Clicking on the link starts a confidential online chat with a crisis specialist. Facebook does not share the names of people who submit suicide reports. If you are not sure what to do, call a suicide hotline and ask for advice about whether or how to intervene.

1. What kind of therapy do you practice?

2. Can you prescribe medication if I need it?

3. Do I need immediate treatment of some kind? What would that treatment involve?

4. Who will know that I am in therapy?

5. Would you recommend group therapy for me?

6. What is the process of the therapy, and what are the goals? How can I achieve them?

7. Will you go over my treatment plan with me?

8. Am I safe from having suicidal thoughts as I have my therapy sessions with you?

9. Can I call, e-mail, or text you between sessions?

10. What should I do if I finish my therapy sessions with you but still feel suicidal?

11. Do you have any good websites or other resources that you can recommend?

10 GREAT QUESTIONS TO ASK A THERAPIST

CHAPTER 5

GETTING TREATMENT

Entering into treatment is extremely valuable for teens who feel suicidal. They need to see therapists, which often requires referrals from their family doctors. Therapists are mental health professionals who design treatment plans for people based on the nature of the problems and the situation in which the young person lives. The plan is made with the individual seeking help and may include regular therapy, medication, or a combination of the two. Therapy is usually conducted on an outpatient basis. Some people who are at high risk for suicide may require hospitalization.

UNDERSTANDING PSYCHOTHERAPY

Often known as talk therapy, psychotherapy is a process in which people talk with mental health professionals about why they feel suicidal and learn healthy ways to help themselves feel better. Individuals who can open up and talk about the disturbing things going in their lives usually find it easier to arrive at positive answers to their problems.

Many different types of psychotherapy exist. Most mental health professionals are trained in several of them. Therapy usually

Therapy provides an opportunity to learn different and healthier ways to perceive and manage negative emotions and to improve interpersonal relationships. This process requires teens to be willing, active participants.

takes the form of guided conversations between the therapists and individuals. Therapists help young people identify troublesome behaviors and negative thoughts and feelings and find out how to make healthy changes. These professionals provide tremendous emotional support and teach coping skills in problem solving and managing anger, stress, and depression.

Individuals usually go to regular weekly sessions with their therapists. Psychotherapy typically runs twelve to twenty weeks, sometimes longer, depending on what young people need and their family's health insurance. For complex issues, such as suicide attempts, treatment could continue for a year or more.

At first, teens may feel angry and uncomfortable discussing their feelings. It can be scary to talk about deeply hidden and powerful emotions as they gain insight into their suicidal thoughts and behavior. Sometimes people become distressed or even cry in sessions or afterward. Learning and applying new ways to solve problems and cope with the ups and downs of daily life requires work and patience. Changing can be somewhat frightening and difficult but also hopeful. The purpose of therapy is to feel better and learn coping skills to handle current and future problems. The vast majority of young people who go through therapy find that it was well worth their effort and time. They feel happier and more confident and in control of their lives after completing therapy.

Types of Therapists

Mental health professionals who provide therapy include psychiatrists, clinical psychologists, clinical social workers, and various types of counselors. Some specialize in treating teens. These professionals often work in clinics, hospitals, or private offices. Most state governments oversee the licensing of mental health professionals, and each state has specific requirements for licensed therapists.

Psychiatrists

Psychiatrists are medical doctors (MDs) with additional training in mental health disorders. They specialize in diagnosing and treating mental, emotional, and behavioral disorders. These doctors can prescribe medicine, order laboratory tests, conduct assessments, and evaluate and treat mental disorders.

Clinical Psychologists

Like psychiatrists, clinical psychologists use different types of therapies to help someone experiencing suicidal thoughts or behaviors. They can also test, diagnose, and treat emotional and behavioral disorders. They cannot prescribe medications. Clinical psychologists have a doctorate degree in psychology (PhD or PsyD).

Clinical Social Workers

Clinical social workers have a master's degree in social work (MSW) and additional training and experience in diagnosing and treating emotional disorders. They usually work in schools, mental health clinics, and private practice.

Counselors

Many kinds of counselors work with teens. Students receive help from school counselors on specific situations, such as educational or job matters. Addiction counselors take special training and certification to assist individuals, including youth, who abuse alcohol or other drugs. Religious counselors are trained to work with people who have mental and social problems.

TYPES OF PSYCHOTHERAPY

Young people frequently find that psychotherapy is extremely valuable for sorting out suicidal feelings and other emotional issues. During this process, therapists talk with teens to help them pinpoint what is making them feel sad, helpless, or hopeless. These professionals help young people identify unique strong points within themselves that they can use to get through difficult times and manage the changes of daily living. Teens learn positive ways to deal with their problems.

Successful therapy depends on various factors. This includes the therapist's empathy (understanding of another person's problems), the motivation and psychological strengths of the teen, and the quality of the relationship between the young person and therapist. Most important is the ability of the therapist and individual to work together. It's immensely important that you build a trusting relationship with a therapist who is a good fit for you.

Psychotherapy is a private process that often involves talking about very sensitive issues. Therapists respect the privacy of minors (under age eighteen) and keep things they are told confidential. Unless young people give permission, therapists will not tell parents, guardians, or other people about what is said during sessions. However, if teens are at imminent risk of harming themselves or someone else, therapists are legally required to report this information to authorities. They must also

CHOOSING A THERAPIST

Good therapists take the problems of teens with suicidal thoughts or behaviors seriously. Before entering into therapy, a young person must be sure he or she can work with a particular therapist. It's a good idea to meet with a few therapists before choosing one. The most important question to ask is whether they have experience treating teens with suicidal behaviors. You should inquire about their training, certification, and experience. Therapists will usually ask how you are feeling emotionally and physically and why you are in therapy. They will talk about the kind of therapy they do, how sessions are run, and what to expect. You should choose a therapist who is respectful of you and gives you hope that you can feel better.

disclose physical or sexual abuse. During the first session, teens should ask the therapist about the level of privacy and confidentiality they can expect.

Sometimes individuals use counseling and psychotherapy as interchangeable terms, but they really aren't the same. Counselors in school, for example, usually give advice to students about short-term practical matters. A teen may feel uncomfortable telling someone he or she is seeing a therapist. If so, it's okay to substitute "counselor" for "therapist" when talking with family, friends, or other people.

Psychodynamic Psychotherapy (Insight-Oriented Therapy)

Psychodynamic psychotherapy, also known as insight-oriented therapy, helps young people look at their unconscious emotional issues. During therapy, teens who are suicidal explore their beliefs, events, and feelings. They often discover that their patterns of relating to others do not work well or are unhealthy. By having a better understanding of their responses in difficult relationships, young people can develop helpful behaviors. They can then use their positive skills to successfully interact with people.

Cognitive Behavioral Therapy (CBT)

Cognitive behavioral therapy (CBT) helps individuals change negative thoughts (cognition) that are causing them problems in particular situations, which then alters the way they feel and act. Many suicidal teens have a negative view of themselves and the world, and they feel helpless and hopeless about their future. Through CBT, they learn to identify undesirable beliefs and actions and replace them with positive, healthy ones. Teens feel better and behave differently in response to life stresses, even when their circumstances stay the same.

Family Therapy

In this approach, the entire family learns how to cope with problems by working together. Therapists help them develop better communications, resolve family conflicts, and promote family bonds. In addition, young people see that their families care about them, which can help protect them from suicidal behaviors.

Group Treatment

Group therapy brings teens who are struggling with similar issues together to share experiences and provide support for each other. It also allows them

Individual therapy is when a therapist works with a teen one-on-one. Sometimes all members of a family, including parents or guardians, will meet with a therapist in family therapy in a private room.

to practice new coping strategies and problem-solving skills with peers. Therapists supervise these groups.

Treatment with Medications

Many people who have suicidal thoughts and behaviors are depressed. Agreeing to take an antidepressant is a strong step forward in dealing with their depression. Doctors frequently prescribe antidepressant medications to lift mood and lower the risk of suicide. They may also prescribe antianxiety medicines or other drugs. Drug therapy alone may provide enough support for young people who feel suicidal. However, a combination of psychotherapy and medicines usually works best.

Treatment with medications takes time and patience. Sometimes teens need to try several medications before they find what works well. In addition, antidepressants need a few weeks or longer to begin affecting mood. Individuals may notice their thoughts are less negative and clearer, their sleep is better, and they feel better during this time. Antidepressants can take six to eight weeks to be fully effective.

Some of the possible side effects of antidepressants may seem worrisome, but they vary widely from person to person. Teens may experience no side effects, while others have only minor discomfort. Side effects often lessen or disappear within four weeks or so of beginning antidepressants. The great majority of these drugs are generally safe. However, teens and young adults may have an increase in suicidal thoughts or behavior when taking antidepressants, especially in the first few

Antidepressants don't dramatically make people different. Instead, these prescription medications positively change certain aspects of how people think, feel, and act, which helps them take better care of themselves.

weeks after starting or when the dose is changed. They must be closely monitored during this time. It's important to remember that antidepressants are much more likely to reduce suicide risk in the long run by improving mood.

BRIEF CRISIS-ORIENTED TREATMENT

Schools and clinics usually offer short-term crisis counseling for teens experiencing suicidal behavior. This type of counseling provides quick, immediate assistance and usually lasts three to six weeks. It helps young people learn to minimize stress and provides them with emotional support. Sessions may focus on problem-solving or coping skills and sometimes require parents to attend.

Crisis treatment alone is usually inadequate to treat the underlying problems that put the young person at risk for suicide. Someone who is depressed and suicidal requires ongoing mental health care. Hospitalization may be necessary if the individual's life is at high risk. Usually, crisis treatment is short-term.

HOSPITALIZATION

People in a terrible crisis may believe that suicide is a fast way to end their despair. However, their suicide attempts may not get the result they want. If individuals seriously harm themselves, they may end up in a hospital emergency room with damage to their bodies that cannot be fixed.

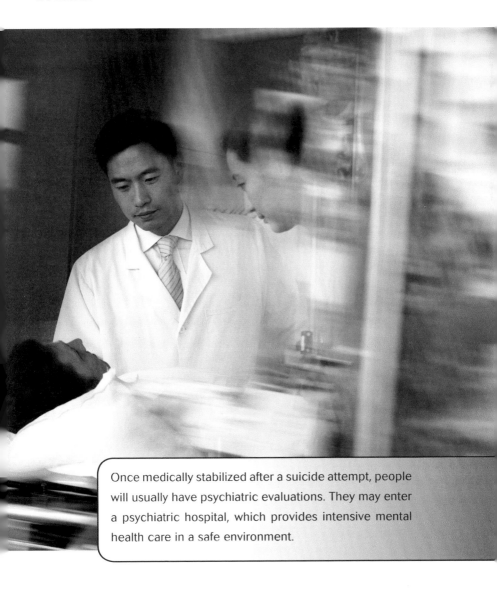

Once medically stabilized after a suicide attempt, people will usually have psychiatric evaluations. They may enter a psychiatric hospital, which provides intensive mental health care in a safe environment.

When individuals are hospitalized because of a suicide attempt, the emergency medical staff will first treat the physical problems. After that, it's important for young people to tell the health professionals whether they truly wanted to end their life, did not care if they lived or died, or had other reasons for their actions. Being honest helps teens receive the right type of mental health treatment. Hospitalization may be best if a person is seriously thinking about suicide or taking definite steps toward ending his or her life. Professionals closely monitor patients and usually provide psychotherapy every day one-on-one and in groups. Sometimes family members attend sessions with their teens.

CHAPTER 6

Teens who experience suicidal thoughts often find that taking a doctor's prescribed antidepressant(s) and having therapy stabilizes their moods and helps relieve symptoms of depression. As they work with their therapists, they begin to learn and use effective ways to cope with emotional problems. Most people recover from suicide attempts and overcome their feelings of despair and hopelessness. Positive steps toward recovery include being responsible for treatment, making an action plan, managing stress, and developing a healthy lifestyle.

It's not easy to change behavior, especially when confronted with emotions and memories that have previously triggered suicidal thoughts. Teens cannot change their past, but they can influence what happens moving forward.

FOLLOWING YOUR TREATMENT PLAN

Actively participating in your own treatment helps you feel better and take control of your life. It's essential to stick with and follow the plan you and your therapist design. Young people will gain the most from their therapy by actively participating in the sessions, doing any homework exercises, keeping all appointments, and letting the therapist know if something isn't working.

In addition, teens need to take their medications as prescribed and notify their doctors if they begin using over-the-counter or nonprescription drugs. They should continue taking their medications at the same dose even after their symptoms start to improve. Keeping a regular sleep cycle helps maintain a stable level of medication in the body. It's crucial to avoid alcohol and illegal drugs because they worsen depression and increase suicidal thoughts.

A HOTLINES CARD

Therapists recommend that teens make a hotlines card or list in case they or friends have thoughts of harming themselves. This item takes just a little time to create, and then it's available if needed. A hotlines card can be written on an index card, piece of paper, card stock, or anything else that can be easily kept on an individual.

HOTLINES

911 _____
Fire Department _____
Police _____
Crisis lines _____

_____

Hospital Emergency _____

_____

Sometimes teens find that symptoms of serious depression can reappear or stressful situations may trigger thoughts of suicide. An important form of suicide prevention is creating a hotlines card.

People can use the Internet to find and add the telephone numbers to the card. Once completed, teens can make copies of the list and put one near their home telephone and keep a card in their purse, backpack, or wallet. Everyone should also program the emergency numbers into his or her phone and laptop.

DEVELOPING A SELF-CARE PLAN

To deal with reoccurrences of suicidal thoughts, individuals can work with their therapists to write a self-care or action plan and have it ready to use. This plan outlines five steps individuals can take to manage, cope with, and distract from intense negative feelings that can occur at times.

1. To start, teens write down their triggers, which are situations or events that can cause them distress and lead to suicidal thoughts. Some triggers could be a lower-than-anticipated test score, a big fight with a parent or close friend, or the breakup of a romantic relationship.
2. Next, they list warning signs that indicate changes in thoughts, feelings, and behaviors, such as avoiding friends and family, not exercising, or forgetting to take medications or keep therapy appointments.
3. The third step is explaining what they can do when warning signs appear.
4. Teens now make a list of three to five supportive people to contact.
5. Finally, they write some ways to calm themselves, such as playing the guitar, painting, drawing, calling or visiting a supportive relative, listening to upbeat music, walking, running, or bicycling.

CREATE A CHECKLIST

☐ Contact my doctors

Therapist: Dr. Eloise Empfield   Phone: _____

Psychiatrist: Dr. Ryan Chun   Phone: _____

☐ Start each day by writing an affirmation, something for which I am grateful, and a power question.

☐ Do my exercise routines.

☐ Get 8 to 9 hours of sleep every night and eat healthy meals.

☐ Take my medications as prescribed every day.

☐ Check every morning for appointments that day.

☐ Other _____

_____

Having a checklist with specific names and numbers—as well as reminders of daily rituals—is a fast and effective way to ensure that you accomplish your goals and, if necessary, be in touch with your physicians when you need them most.

STRESS MANAGEMENT

At the end of a busy school day, two friends may look at each other and say, "I'm stressed out," or "I feel so stressed right now!" Stress is how the body and mind react to everyday problems and challenges. Most people think of stress as a negative thing, but that's not always true. Stress can have positive effects. For example, teens may get a little nervous before taking a test at school and react by becoming alert and focused on performing well. It can help individuals reach their goals because they feel motivated, excited, energized, and hopeful.

Chronic negative stress, however, can adversely affect sleep, heart rate, digestion, the skin, weight, mood, and memory. To manage responses to stress, teens can use relaxation methods, including deep breathing, muscle relaxation, meditation, and stretching. One simple technique is to sit or stand quietly and concentrate on taking deep breaths for a few minutes. Some people use visualization, in which they think about a peaceful image or relaxing

Humor inspires hope, connects people to each other, and helps keep them focused and alert. Here, Hillary Clinton shares a laugh with Jon Stewart on his TV show, *The Daily Show with Jon Stewart*.

place. Laughter is a fantastic stress reliever! Laughing causes the brain to release feel-good endorphins, which calm tension in the body.

Another way to positively handle emotions is with mindful practices, such as yoga, tai chi, and qui gong. Many people find these exercises mentally and physically helpful because they require mindfulness, meaning they need to focus and think carefully about what their bodies are doing. The quiet movements slow down the heart rate and increase blood and oxygen flow throughout the body, which helps diffuse feelings of stress, sadness, or anxiety. Learning to be in the present in a nonjudgmental way is also mindfulness. Living mindfully allows people to let each moment be just as it is.

Meditation can help reduce stress, regulate emotions, improve focus, and lower blood pressure. Some schools provide meditation training for students. Teens can also learn different techniques from information on the Internet.

POSITIVE LIFESTYLE STRATEGIES

Following a healthy lifestyle helps teens enjoy life and be happy and capable of handling daily challenges. Some simple steps to take are getting enough sleep every night and eating healthy meals and snacks that include whole grains, vegetables, and fruit. Exercising is another way of taking care of yourself that can improve your outlook on life.

Most people have probably heard about the benefits of regular exercise. Those benefits are real! Getting at least sixty minutes a day of aerobic exercise keeps the body strong and the heart and blood pumping at a steady rate. It improves alertness, productivity, and self-image and helps individuals sleep better. Young people feel happier, too, because it boosts the amount of endorphins, or feel-good chemicals, in the brain. Any kind of enjoyable activity is great, including hiking, jogging, swimming, biking, dancing, full-court basketball, or skiing. Even walking the dog, mowing the lawn, or shoveling snow from a driveway counts as exercise.

Positive psychology, such as affirmations and gratitude, are linked to healthy well-being because it installs positive messages into the mind. People who express these emotions are more optimistic and confident, are happier, and have better social networks. Many individuals take the first few minutes after waking in the morning to write positive thoughts and beliefs in a paper or electronic notebook or journal. Affirmations can be anything you like about yourself, such as "I am

Regular exercise contributes to overall health because it helps teens feel good, look good, and stay strong. People find that exercise breaks are refreshing, boosting both their energy and mood.

determined," "I am a caring friend," "I have the power to change myself," "I learn from challenges," or "I attract positive people into my life." Next, write something you appreciate. Perhaps you are thankful for having a best friend, family pet or clean drinking water, or watching the sun rise or set. Taking these quick but powerful steps puts you in a positive mood to begin the day.

Learning to tolerate distress for a short time can help people in a crisis manage negative emotions and get through rough moments. To unwind, they may want to read, play sports, or watch a funny movie. Young people can listen to upbeat music, sing, play instruments, sketch, paint, take photographs, or enjoy looking at beautiful things such as art or flowers. Just sitting back, shutting one's eyes, and daydreaming about a memorable occasion, such as a hiking or camping trip with friends, can release stress. Reaching out to others by volunteering can decrease contact with events that trigger distress.

Being socially connected with other people is extremely important for staying healthy. Isolation and withdrawal tend to worsen feelings of depression. Because developing and maintaining a social network

Having positive people in your life is one of the best ways to build your self-confidence. In turn, good self-esteem helps you feel optimistic and more comfortable with yourself and others.

can be difficult sometimes, teens can ask family and friends to stay in touch with them. They may also want to go to support groups to talk with peers about problems they share. Spending time with positive people lifts the mood.

FINDING YOUR FUTURE

Writing for *xoJane*, an online magazine aimed at girls and women, Kathleen Stewart recalled that as a teen she often lived in a state of great sadness and despair. She had major screaming fights with her parents, often cried, and slept a lot. Deeply depressed, her thoughts became foggy and muddled. She said, "It's hard to tell someone who hasn't experienced major depression what it's like to be continually falling into blackness, to walk around feeling like a shadow among the 'normal' people around you, to know that you're losing touch with reality but not how to stop it." Kathleen could not put words to her feelings or figure out healthy methods to lessen her emotional pain. Instead, she attempted suicide by overdosing on pills, but she survived. Today, as a social worker, she speaks to young people about her experiences and how she reached out for help. When that happened, she learned that things can change. She tells teens that, "It will get better. Maybe not today, or next year, but one day, it will. You're a strong person. You're going to be okay. I promise, it will get better."

BEING IN THE WORLD

Individuals tend to focus inward when they dwell on their own difficult issues. If they feel overwhelmed with unsolvable problems, they may withdraw from the world around them and shut out family, friends, and other people. As teens continue their treatment and feel better about themselves, they can begin to focus outward and build a healthy lifestyle. Connecting with other people gives everyone a feeling of belonging and that his or her life has a purpose.

Volunteering in your community is a great way to help other people—and yourself. Individuals who donate their time feel more socially connected, engaged, and focused on the present, which wards off depression and loneliness. To look for volunteer opportunities, teens can contact community agencies such as hospitals, clinics, religious organizations, boys' and girls' clubs, and charities. The Internet provides a wealth of information about opportunities, and many local communities have volunteer clearinghouses. Young people may want to help at a crisis clinic. There, they receive professional training and become part of a team that makes a difference in the lives of other people. For example, Teen Link in Washington provides youth suicide prevention. Individuals may volunteer to join the Youth Suicide Speakers Bureau or provide help to troubled individuals who call the Teen Link Help Line.

Many other volunteer opportunities are available. Teens can join clubs that do helpful work in the community, such as reading stories to children in hospital cancer wards or participating in water and river cleanup projects. They might work with the local Red Cross to assemble comfort kits for those in need after a disaster. Some young people have organized community events to collect food and clothing for individuals who have lost their homes because of flood, hurricane, or other natural catastrophes. One way to raise money for a cause is to hold an activity, such as a

car wash, bake sale, walk, run, or bicycle race. To get started, teens can talk to a local supermarket, place of worship, or community center, such as the YMCA.

The vast majority of people who once seriously thought about suicide recover and go on to lead healthy, adaptive lives. Medications keep them functioning well, and therapy helps them learn how to cope with a wide variety of feelings and situations. In turn, these tools assist them when managing the successes, challenges, and opportunities in their current lives and help them stay on the path of wellness and hope.

The Big Brothers Big Sisters program provides healthy relationships for youth aged six to eighteen. Participants are matched with upbeat, caring, and supportive volunteers who help young people develop positively.

GLOSSARY

antidepressant A prescription medication used to treat depression and other disorders, such as anxiety.

assessment An evaluation, usually performed by a physician, of a person's mental, emotional, and social capabilities.

autocide A suicide disguised as an vehicle accident.

bullycide The act of killing oneself because of bullying.

depression A mental illness in which sadness overwhelms a person's life.

diagnosis The identification of an illness following an examination.

hotline A call center staffed by specially trained people to give callers immediate support.

optimism A tendency to view the world positively.

overdose A deadly amount of a drug that can lead to coma or death.

perfectionism An overriding desire to be perfect.

pessimism A tendency to view the world negatively.

psychiatrist A medical doctor who specializes in diagnosing and treating mental, emotional, and behavioral disorders. He or she can prescribe medicine, order laboratory tests, conduct assessments, and evaluate and treat mental disorders.

psychologist An individual who is trained to test, diagnose, and treat emotional and behavioral disorders but cannot prescribe medications.

psychotherapy A treatment that helps people understand their thoughts, feelings, behaviors, and relationships with others.

relaxation techniques Methods used to relax and ease symptoms of distress, such as deep breathing, muscle relaxation, meditation, and stretching.

self-destructive behavior Acting in a way that will harm oneself.

self-esteem Self-confidence; how an individual feels about himself or herself.

stress Mental or physical tension as a response to a condition, situation, or incident.

suicide The intentional act of taking one's own life.

suicide rate The percentage of people in a specific group who take their own lives in a certain period of time.

therapist A person trained to help patients recover from a mental or physical illness or cope with daily life.

therapy Treatment for a disease or condition.

warning signs Specific observable behaviors of an individual in crisis. These symptoms may indicate that the person is at risk of suicide.

FOR MORE INFORMATION

American Association of Suicidology
5221 Wisconsin Avenue NW
Washington, DC 20015
(202) 237-2280
Website: http://www.suicidology.org

The American Association of Suicidology supports research, public awareness and education programs, and training for professionals and volunteers. It is also a national clearinghouse for information on suicide.

American Foundation for Suicide Prevention
120 Wall Street, 29th Floor
New York, NY 10005
(888) 333-2377
Website: http://www.afsp.org

This organization seeks to understand and prevent suicide through research, education, and advocacy. Its website offers extensive information on suicide.

Canadian Association for Suicide Prevention
870 Portage Avenue
Winnipeg, MB R3G 0P1
Canada
(204) 784-4073
Website: http://suicideprevention.ca

The Canadian Association for Suicide Prevention works to reduce the suicide rate and minimize the harmful consequences of suicide through support and education. Its website offers extensive information on suicide across Canada.

Canadian Mental Health Association

1110-151 Slater Street
Ottawa, ON K1P 5H3
Canada
(613) 745-7750
Website: http://www.cmha.ca

This organization promotes the mental health of all people experiencing mental illness through advocacy, education, research, and service.

National Alliance on Mental Illness

3803 N. Fairfax Drive, Suite 100
Arlington, VA 22203
(800) 950-6264
Website: http://www.nami.org

The National Alliance on Mental Illness is the nation's largest nonprofit organization that addresses all aspects of mental illness.

National Organization for People of Color Against Suicide

P.O. Box 75571
Washington, DC 20013
(866) 899-5317
Website: http://nopcas.com

The goal of the National Organization for People of Color Against Suicide seeks to increase suicide education and awareness for communities of color.

Suicide Awareness Voices of Education (SAVE)

8120 Penn Avenue S, Suite 470
Bloomington, MN 55431

(952) 946-7998

Website: http://www.save.org

SAVE works to prevent suicide through public awareness and education and serves as a resource for people touched by suicide.

Suicide Prevention Resource Center

Education Development Center

43 Foundry Avenue

Waltham, MA 02453

(877) 438-7772

Website: http://www.sprc.org

The Suicide Prevention Resource Center provides support, training, and information resources to increase the expertise of professionals who work with people at risk for suicide.

WEBSITES

Because of the changing nature of Internet links, Rosen Publishing has developed an online list of websites related to the subject of this book. This site is updated regularly. Please use this link to access the list:

http://www.rosenlinks.com/411/Sui

FOR FURTHER READING

Agnello, Evonne. *Shaking Shame from Mental Illness.* Bothell, WA: Book Publishers Network, 2012.

Biegel, Gina. *The Stress Reduction Workbook for Teens: Mindfulness Skills to Help You Deal with Stress.* Oakland, CA: Instant Help, 2010.

Ciarrochi, Joseph, and Louise Hayes. *Get Out of Your Mind and Into Your Life for Teens: A Guide to Living an Extraordinary Life.* Oakland, CA: Instant Help, 2012.

Dowrick, Christopher, and Susan Martin. *Can I Tell You About Depression? A Guide for Friends, Family and Professionals.* London, UK: Jessica Kingsley Publishers, 2015.

Esherick, Joan. *Managing Stress.* Broomall, PA: Mason Crest Publishers, 2013.

Esherick, Joan. *Suicide and Self-Destructive Behaviors.* Broomall, PA: Mason Crest Publishers, 2013.

Fonda, Jane. *Being a Teen: Everything Teen Girls and Boys Should Know About Relationships, Sex, Love, Health, Identity & More.* St. Louis, MO: Turtleback Books, 2014.

Fox, Marci, and Leslie Sokol. *Think Confident, Be Confident for Teens: A Cognitive Therapy Guide to Overcoming Self-Doubt and Creating Unshakable Self-Esteem.* Oakland, CA: Instant Help, 2011.

Hines, Kevin. *Cracked, Not Broken: Surviving and Thriving After a Suicide Attempt.* Lanham, MD: Rowman & Littlefield Publishers, 2013.

Huddele, Lorena, and Jay Schleifer. *Teen Suicide*. New York, NY: Rosen Publishing, 2011.

Lesoine, Robert, and Marilynne Chopel. *Unfinished Conversation: Healing from Suicide and Loss*. Berkeley, CA: Parallax Press, 2013.

Lohmann, Raychelle, and Julia V. Taylor. *The Bullying Workbook for Teens: Activities to Help You Deal with Social Aggression and Cyberbullying*. Oakland, CA: Instant Help, 2013.

Love, Angerona S. *When Darkness Comes: Saying "No" to Suicide*. Louisville, KY: Insight Solutions, 2010.

Marcovitz, Hal. *Teens and Suicide*. Broomall, PA: Mason Crest, 2013.

Miller, Craig A. *This Is How It Feels: A Memoir, Attempting Suicide and Finding Life*. Seattle, WA: CreateSpace Independent Publishing, 2012.

Peterson, Judy M. *How to Beat Cyberbullying*. New York, NY: Rosen Publishing, 2013.

Press, Elisha. *Mindfulness Made Simple: An Introduction to Finding Calm Through Mindfulness and Meditation*. Kelseyville, CA: Calistoga Press, 2014.

Robinson, Antwala. *YOU Rule! Take Charge of Your Health and Life: A Healthy Lifestyle Guide for Teens*. Atlanta, GA: Wellness Agent, 2014.

Schab, Lisa M. *The Self-Esteem Workbook for Teens: Activities to Help You Build Confidence and Achieve Your Goals*. Oakland, CA: Instant Help, 2013.

Schwartz, Tina P. *Depression: The Ultimate Teen Guide*. Lanham, MD: Rowman & Littlefield Publishers, 2014.

Smith, Tom. *The Unique Grief of Suicide: Questions and Hope*. Bloomington, IN: iUniverse, 2013.

Stillman, Sarah. *Soul Searching: A Girl's Guide to Finding Herself*. New York, NY: Simon Pulse/ Beyond Words, 2012.

Van Dijk, Sheri. *Don't Let Your Emotions Run Your Life for Teens*. Oakland, CA: Instant Help, 2011.

BIBLIOGRAPHY

Berman, Alan L., David A. Jobes, and Morton M. Silverman. *Adolescent Suicide: Assessment and Intervention*. Washington, DC: American Psychological Association, 2006.

Bertini, Kristine. *Understanding and Preventing Suicide: The Development of Self-Destructive Patterns and Ways to Alter Them*. Westport, CT: Praeger Publishers, 2009.

CBSNews.com. "Study Pinpoints When People Are Most Likely to Commit Suicide." June 3, 2014. Retrieved September 2, 2014 (http://www .cbsnews.com/news/study-pinpoints-when-people -are-most-likely-to-commit-suicide).

Cunningham, Amy, and Heidi Bryan. "Creating a Safety Plan." 2014. Retrieved September 1, 2014 (http://www.suicidefindinghope.com/content /creating_a_safety_plan).

Dobbs, David. "Clues in the Cycle of Suicide." *New York Times*, June 24, 2013. Retrieved September 9, 2014 (http://well.blogs.nytimes.com /2013/06/24/clues-in-the-cycle-of-suicide).

Elgazzar, Kareem. "Wyoming Teen Recounts Three Suicide Attempts Since He Was 8, Hopeful His Story Can Help Others." WCPO Cincinnati, August 5, 2013. Retrieved January 8, 2014 (http://www.wcpo.com/news/local-news/

wyoming-teen-recounts-three-suicide-attempts -since-he-was-8-hopeful-his-story-can-help-others).

Joiner, Thomas. *Why People Die by Suicide.* Cambridge, MA: Harvard University Press, 2005.

King, Cheryl A., Cynthia Ewell Foster, and Kelly M. Rogalaski. *Teen Suicide Risk: A Practitioner Guide to Screening, Assessment, and Management.* New York, NY: Guilford Press, 2013.

Machoian, Lisa. *The Disappearing Girl: Learning the Language of Teenage Depression.* New York, NY: Plume, 2006.

Marcus, Eric. *Why Suicide? Questions and Answers About Suicide, Suicide Prevention, and Coping with the Suicide of Someone You Know.* New York, NY: HarperOne, 2010.

Mondimore, Francis Mark. *Adolescent Depression: A Guide for Parents.* Baltimore, MD: Johns Hopkins University Press, 2002.

Serani, Deborah. *Living with Depression: Why Biology and Biography Matter Along the Path to Hope and Happiness.* Lanham, MD: Rowman and Littlefield Publishing Group, 2012.

Smith, Melinda, Jeanne Segal, and Lawrence Robinson. "Suicide Prevention: How to Help Someone Who Is Suicidal." September 2014. Retrieved September 10, 2014 (http://www .helpguide.org/articles/suicide-prevention /suicide-prevention-helping-someone-who-is -suicidal.htm).

Stewart, Kathleen. "I Survived a Teenage Suicide Attempt or Why We Must Talk About Suicide." *xoJane*, November 2, 2012. Retrieved January 10, 2015 (http://www.xojane.com/it-happened-to-me /it-happened-to-me-i-survived-a-teenage-suicide -attempt).

Suicide Prevention Resource Center. "Suicide Risk and Prevention for Lesbian, Gay, Bisexual, and Transgender Youth." 2008. Retrieved August 10, 2014 (http://www.sprc.org/sites/sprc.org/files /library/SPRC_LGBT_Youth.pdf).

Taffet, David. "Elliott's Story: How 1 Teen Survived Bullying, Suicide Attempt." *Dallas Voice*, January 10, 2015. Retrieved January 11, 2015 (http://www .dallasvoice.com/elliotts-story-1-teen-survived -bullying-suicide-attempt-1047577.html).

U.S. Centers for Disease Control and Prevention. "Sexual Identity, Sex of Sexual Contacts, and Health-Risk Behaviors Among Students in Grades 9–12. Youth Risk Behavior Surveillance, Selected Sites, United States, 2001–2009." June 6, 2011. Retrieved August 4, 2014 (http://www.cdc.gov/mmwr/pdf/ss /ss60e0606.pdf).

U.S. Centers for Disease Control and Prevention. "Suicide: The Facts." 2012. Retrieved August 9, 2014 (http://www.cdc.gov/violenceprevention/ pdf/suicidc_datasheet-a.pdf).

U.S. Centers for Disease Control and Prevention. "Suicides Due to Alcohol and/or Drug Overdose:

A Data Brief from the National Violent Death
Reporting System" 2013. Retrieved August 12,
2014 (http://www.cdc.gov/violenceprevention
/pdf/NVDRS_Data_Brief-a.pdf).

World Health Organization. "Preventing Suicide: A
Global Imperative." 2014. Retrieved August 6,
2014 (http://www.who.int/mental_health
/suicide-prevention/world_report_2014/en).

INDEX

About the Author

Judy Monroe Peterson has earned two master's degrees and is the author of more than seventy educational books for young people, including books on many health and life skills topics. She is a former health care, technical, and academic librarian and college faculty member, biologist, and research scientist. She has taught courses at 3M, the University of Minnesota, and Lake Superior College.

Photo Credits

Cover, p. 1 © iStockphoto.com/drbimages; p. 5 Jupiter Images/Stockbyte/ Thinkstock; pp. 8–9, 58–59, 67, 90–91 Monkey Business Images/ Shutterstock.com; pp. 10–11 Age-standardized suicide rates (per 100,000 population) both sexes, 2012, World Health Organization, © WHO 2014. http://gamapserver.who.int/mapLibrary/Files/Maps/Global_AS_suicide _rates_bothsexes_2012.png; pp. 13, 40 CDC Division of Violence Prevention, http://www.cdc.gov/violenceprevention/suicide/statistics/youth _risk.html, http://www.cdc.gov/violenceprevention/suicide/statistics/rates03 .html; pp. 14–15 New York Times Co./Neal Boenzi/Archive Photos/Getty Images; p. 17 Axente Vlad/Shutterstock.com; pp. 22–23 The Washington Post/Getty Images; p. 25 Stockbyte/Thinkstock; pp. 26–27 SpeedKingz/ Shutterstock.com; p. 29 Stockbyte/Getty Images; pp. 30–31 prudkov/iStock/ Thinkstock; p. 35 Photolibrary/Getty Images; pp. 44–45 E+/Getty Images; p. 48 Saša Prudkov/iStock/Thinkstock; pp. 52–53, 84–85 © AP Images; pp. 54–55 Stephen Lovekin/Getty Images; pp. 62–63 Rudyanto Wijaya/ iStock/Thinkstock; p. 73 Lisa F. Young/Shutterstock.com; p. 75 Jason Stitt/ Shutterstock.com; pp. 76–77 XiXinXing/iStock/Thinkstock; p. 79 Purestock/ Thinkstock; pp. 86–87 takayuki/Shutterstock.com; p. 89 Mike Cherim/ iStock/Thinkstock; pp. 94–95 Eyecandy Images/Thinkstock.

Designer: Les Kanturek; Executive Editor: Hope Lourie Killcoyne; Editor: Meredith Day